I Made It!

Process-Oriented Art for Kids

About This Book

From blending and dipping to rolling and wrapping, you'll find a whole lot of fun woven into one book with *I Made It!* You'll find 20 unique art techniques and 60 different hands-on activities adapted from *The Mailbox®* line of books and magazines. These process-oriented activities put artistic expression right in the hands of your pint-size Picassos!

Each conveniently organized section highlights one technique and includes three different art activities focusing on the featured process. Each activity includes

- a brief materials list
- simple step-by-step directions for setting up the activity and for guiding students through the process-oriented activity
- ideas for enhancing or extending the process or resulting project

We've also included some nifty display ideas for you to exhibit students' resulting masterpieces!

Managing Editor: Allison E. Ward
Editor at Large: Diane Badden
Staff Editors: Cindy K. Daoust, Susan Walker
Copy Editors: Tazmen Carlisle, Amy Kirtley-Hill, Karen L. Mayworth, Kristy Parton, Debbie Shoffner, Cathy Edwards Simrell
Art Coordinator: Donna K. Teal
Artists: Pam Crane, Theresa Lewis Goode, Clevell Harris, Ivy L. Koonce, Clint Moore, Greg D. Rieves, Rebecca Saunders, Barry Slate, Stuart Smith, Donna K. Teal
Cover Artist: Ivy L. Koonce
The Mailbox® Books.com: Judy P. Wyndham (MANAGER); Jennifer Tipton Bennett (DESIGNER/ARTIST); Karen White (INTERNET COORDINATOR); Paul Fleetwood, Xiaoyun Wu (SYSTEMS)

President, The Mailbox Book Company™: Joseph C. Bucci
Director of Book Planning and Development: Chris Poindexter
Curriculum Director: Karen P. Shelton
Book Development Managers: Cayce Guiliano, Elizabeth H. Lindsay, Thad McLaurin
Editorial Planning: Kimberley Bruck (MANAGER); Debra Liverman, Sharon Murphy, Susan Walker (TEAM LEADERS)
Editorial and Freelance Management: Karen A. Brudnak; Sarah Hamblet, Hope Rodgers (EDITORIAL ASSISTANTS)
Editorial Production: Lisa K. Pitts (TRAFFIC MANAGER); Lynette Dickerson (TYPE SYSTEMS); Mark Rainey (TYPESETTER)
Librarian: Dorothy C. McKinney

What Is Process-Oriented Art?

Process-oriented art focuses on the process of art, not cookie-cutter outcomes. It invites students to think about and explore technique and medium, as well as their own creative self-expression! The activities in this book include a wide variety of materials and a wide range of experiences, resulting in open-ended outcomes. Planning and using process-oriented art activities such as these will help foster a lifelong love of art and the creative process.

Easy Art Tips

Use the tips below to help your students get the most from their art experience!

Getting Started

- All of the projects are easy to do, but it's a good idea to try them out first.

- Do a little upfront thinking about how you will carry out the activity with your children.

- It's a good idea to enlist the help of parents. Send students home with a letter requesting needed materials. Repeat the letter whenever supplies are running low or you need a specific item. Also ask for volunteers as desired. Art is for everyone!

- Gather all your materials and set up the activity as directed. Then follow the simple steps of the process and see where it takes you!

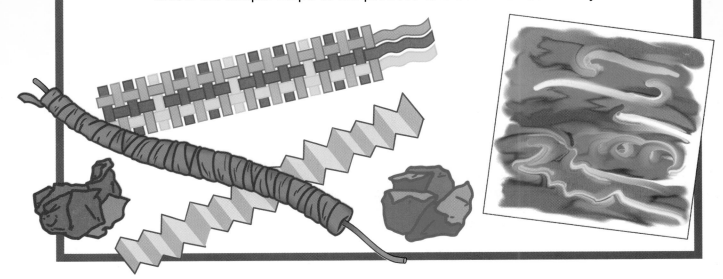

Clever Cover-Ups and Cleanups

- Whatever your workspace of choice, be sure to cover it up. Creating art is a fun but messy process! Use newspaper, old sheets, towels, tablecloths, or shower curtains to protect workspaces and surrounding areas.

- No young artist can resist a cool cover-up. Any old garments—shirts, pants, and socks—serve the purpose of protecting students and their clothing. Add these items to the supply request letter suggested in "Getting Started," and you will be good to go!

- Have lots of damp sponges, towels, or paper towels handy for easy cleanup of messy spills and splatters.

Safety First!

- Students are working with a wide variety of materials! Be sure to properly supervise them.

Drawing Out the Art Experience

- As students work, ask open-ended questions to stimulate their thinking and the creative process.

- Encourage your little ones to give input about their preferences. They will have more fun learning about techniques, mediums, and colors that interest them.

Grand Finales

- Celebrate! Have special art exhibitions where your young artists share their work and their feelings about the creative process.

- Be creative! Highlight students' work in a special art area that changes with the change in process, or fill your classroom with a variety of projects representing a variety of processes.

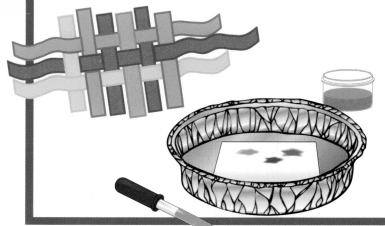

Blend a Rainbow

Transform primary colors with this beautiful blending technique!

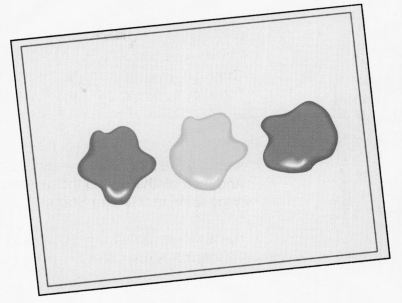

Materials:
- class supply of 9" x 12" sheets of white construction paper
- red, yellow, and blue fingerpaint
- plastic spoons
- class supply of 10" x 13" sheets of waxed paper

Setup:
1. Place a plastic spoon in each jar of fingerpaint.
2. Arrange the materials for easy student access.

Process:
Have each child follow these steps to use the blending process:
1. Drop a spoonful of each color of paint onto your construction paper. Make sure the paint drops are in a line and close together.
2. Cover the paint with waxed paper.
3. Blend the paint by rubbing and pressing the waxed paper.
4. Carefully peel off the waxed paper and throw it away.
5. Set the construction paper aside to dry.

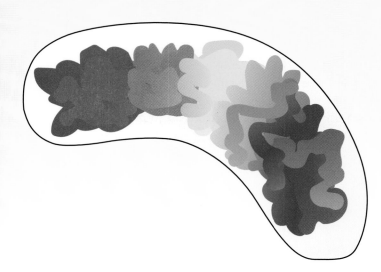

Finishing Touches

Encourage youngsters to notice the rainbow of colors created by the blending process. Then invite each child to draw and cut out a rainbow shape from her paper. If desired, display the rainbows on a bulletin board titled "Razzle-Dazzle Rainbows."

Blending

Pretty Hearts

Swirling, spreading, mixing colors are sure to blend well with your youngsters' art interests!

Materials:
- class supply of 9" x 12" sheets of white construction paper
- water-filled spray bottle
- various colors of thinned tempera paint
- paintbrushes (one for each color of paint)

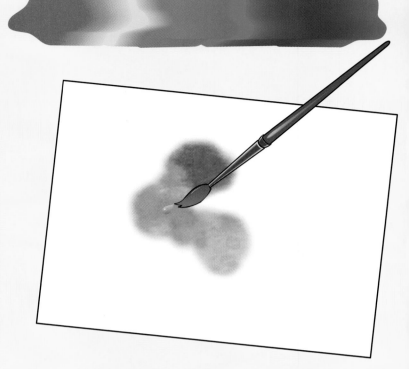

Setup:
Arrange the materials for easy student access.

Process:
Have each child follow these steps to use the blending process:
1. Spray water onto your sheet of paper to dampen it.
2. Use a paintbrush to drop on small puddles of paint. Use several different colors.
3. Blend the paint by allowing the colors to spread and mix together.
4. Create different effects by adding more paint, tilting the paper, or spraying more water.
5. Place the paper on a flat surface to dry.

Finishing Touches

This sweetheart of a project is easy, pretty, and fun! Have each child use a black marker to draw hearts on her paper. Then have her loosely cut around the outlines. Mount the heart cutouts on construction paper and display them in your classroom. What a lovely touch!

Blending

Tropical Sunset

Escape to the islands with this warm blended sunset.

Materials:
- class supply of 9" x 12" sheets of white construction paper
- red, yellow, and orange fingerpaint
- 3 plastic teaspoons

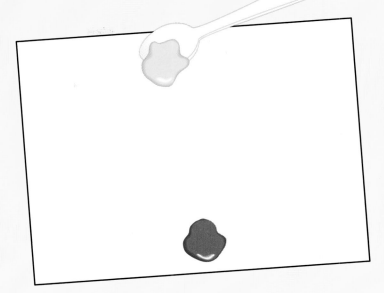

Setup:
1. Place a plastic spoon in each jar of fingerpaint.
2. Arrange the materials for easy student access.

Process:
Have each child follow these steps to use the blending process:
1. Think about sunsets and the colors you see in them. Then choose two colors of paint that you'd like to use to make a sunset.
2. Drop one spoonful of paint near the top of your construction paper. Drop a spoonful of the other color near the bottom of your paper.
3. Spread the paint with your fingers so that the colors blend in the middle of the paper. Work the paint until you are happy with the sunset, adding more paint if needed.
4. Place the construction paper on a flat surface to dry.

Finishing Touches

For a tropical touch, why not add islands to the sunsets? Invite each child to use black tempera paint, an oval sponge, and a palm tree–shaped sponge to make prints on his paper. Looking at these projects, you can almost hear hula music in the breeze!

Blowing

Windy Art

When the wind picks up, invite it into your classroom for some blustery paint fun!

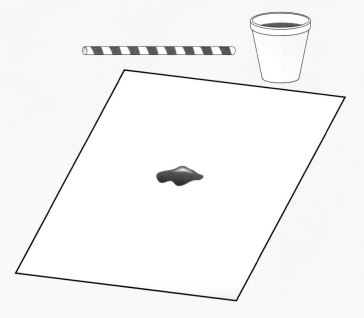

Materials:
- class supply of white construction paper
- thinned tempera paint in a variety of colors
- class supply of straws

Setup:
Arrange the materials for easy student access.

Process:
Have each child follow these steps to use the blowing process:
1. Think about how the wind blows things around outside. Then pretend to be the wind while you blow to paint a picture.
2. Drop a blob of paint in the center of your construction paper.
3. Use a straw to blow the paint around your paper.
4. Place the construction paper on a flat surface to dry.

Finishing Touches

When the paint is dry, consider extending the fun by encouraging each child to repeatedly draw around the design. Mount each page on a colorful, larger sheet of construction paper; then display the resulting projects. What a breeze!

Bubbly Mural

Blowing bubbles has never been more interesting!

Materials:
- length of white bulletin board paper
- several containers of bubble solution with wands.
- food coloring

Setup:

1. Color each container of bubble solution by mixing in several drops of food coloring. Repeat with various colors as desired.
2. Tape the paper to a low section of wall.
3. Arrange the colored bubble solutions for easy student access.

Process:

Have each child follow these steps to use the blowing process:

1. Choose a color of bubble solution.
2. Blow bubbles onto the paper on the wall.
3. Watch the bubbles appear as they hit the paper and pop.
4. Repeat Steps 2–3 with another color of bubble solution.

Finishing Touches

When the mural is dry, why not have each child write her initials inside a bubble? Then display it in your classroom as a reminder of your bubbly youngsters. Bet they'll be bursting with pride!

Ping-Pong Paintings

Little ones will huff and they'll puff and they'll blow this ball around!

Materials:

- length of bulletin board paper
- cup each of red, yellow, and blue tempera paint
- 3 Ping-Pong balls
- 3 plastic spoons
- class supply of drinking straws

Setup:

1. Tape the paper to a low table.
2. Put one ball into each cup of paint and place the cups near the paper-covered table.
3. Help students choose partners for this activity.
4. Arrange the straws for easy student access.

Process:

Have each pair of students follow these steps to use the blowing process:

1. Choose a color of paint.
2. Use a spoon to remove a ball from a paint cup and place it on the paper.
3. Stand on the opposite side of the table as your partner.
4. Blow through a straw to move the ball toward your partner. Have him blow through his straw to send the ball back.
5. Continue in this manner for several passes. Then put the ball back into its cup.

Finishing Touches

If desired, cut the dried painting into shapes to correspond with your current classroom theme. Have a ball with these displays!

Brush

Tissue Painting

Youngsters will eagerly give tissue paper the brush-off once they explore this cool process!

Materials:
- poster board squares in a variety of sizes
- 1" squares of various colors of tissue paper
- water
- vinegar
- plastic containers
- paintbrushes

Setup:
1. Mix equal parts water and vinegar to make transfer liquid. Put containers of the solution along with paintbrushes on a table.
2. Arrange the poster board and tissue paper squares for easy student access.

Process:
Have each pair of students follow these steps to use the brushing process:
1. Brush transfer liquid all over the dull side of your poster board square to wet it.
2. Put a tissue paper square on your poster board. Brush more liquid over it.
3. Continue placing and brushing over tissue paper until the poster board is completely covered.
4. Let the poster board dry overnight.
5. Brush off the tissue squares.

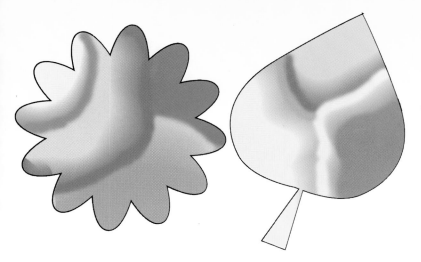

Finishing Touches

Why not take a botanist's approach to display this colorful process? Invite students to draw and cut out leaves and flowers from their dried poster board squares. Hang them around your room for a pretty garden effect.

rushing

A Colorful Creation

Wide, narrow, smooth, rough—the right brush makes all the difference!

Materials:

- class supply of 12" x 18" construction paper
- variety of inexpensive paintbrushes (foam brushes, watercolor brushes, housepainting brushes, chip brushes, etc.)
- tempera paint
- containers of rinse water

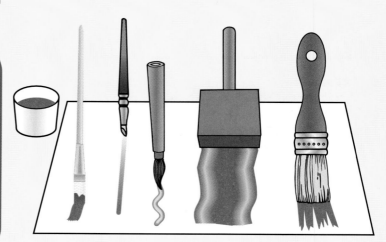

Setup:

Arrange the materials for easy student access.

Process:

Have each child follow these steps to use the brushing process:

1. Look at the different types of brushes. Notice the differences.
2. Choose a brush. Dip it into some paint and stroke it across your paper. What mark does it make? What do the edges look like?
3. Rinse the brush for the next person.
4. Repeat Steps 2 and 3 until you've tried lots of paintbrushes. Then pick your favorite and paint a smiley face with it.

Finishing Touches

When each child's painting is dry, gather students and have them group the paintings by matching each paintbrush with its smiley faces. If desired, have each child trim around his smiley face and mount it on a bulletin board with the matching brush. Title the resulting board "Brushing Up on Painting!" Invite students to refer to the board when painting to determine the effects of each type of brush. How handy!

Brushing

Stroke, Stroke, Stroke

Little ones will really enjoy experimenting with brushstrokes and color!

Materials:
- black construction paper
- white tempera paint
- various other colors of tempera paint
- plastic spoons
- paintbrushes in a variety of sizes and textures

Setup:
1. Put a spoon into each container of paint and then place the containers in your art area.
2. Arrange the brushes and construction paper for easy student access.

Process:
Have each pair of students follow these steps to use the brushing technique:
1. Put one spoonful of white paint on your paper.
2. Put one spoonful of a different color of paint on your paper.
3. Choose a paintbrush. Use it to move the paint on your paper. Make long strokes, short strokes, squiggles, and swirls.
4. Let the paint dry.

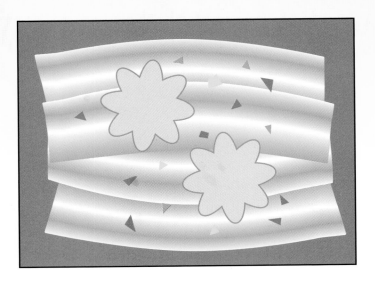

Finishing Touches

This open-ended brushing technique really lends itself to collage. While the paint is still wet, invite each child to sprinkle his painting with glitter, confetti, and small seasonal cutouts. When the paint is dry, mount each resulting project on a larger sheet of colorful construction paper. It's perfect for any occasion!

Crumpling

Frame It!

These fabulous frames will inspire your young artists any time of year!

Materials:
- class set of 6" tagboard squares
- head-and-shoulder school photo of each child
- assorted supply of tissue paper pieces
- glue
- Mod Podge sealant
- paintbrush
- magnetic tape

Setup:
Arrange the tagboard squares, photos, tissue paper, and glue for easy student access.

Process:
Have each child follow these steps to use the crumpling process:

1. Find your photo and glue it to the center of a tagboard square.
2. Scrunch and crumple tissue paper pieces and glue each to the tagboard to frame your photo. *(You may want to plan more than one sitting to ensure a thorough job.)*
3. Let your project dry overnight.
4. On another day, paint a layer of Mod Podge sealant over the project and set it aside to dry.
5. Attach a piece of magnetic tape to the back.

Finishing Touches

Encourage each child to give his framed photo to a loved one. Mom, Dad, or grandparents would be eager recipients of this highly photogenic art!

Crumpling

From Crumpled to Creative

Who would guess that scrunched tissue paper squares could be so beautiful!

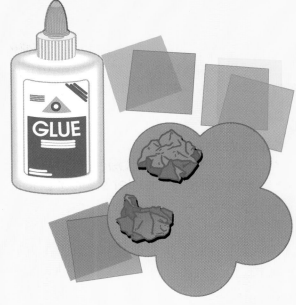

Materials:
- assorted colors of 4" tissue paper squares
- class supply of 9" x 12" construction paper
- glue
- scissors (optional)

Setup:

Arrange the materials for easy student access.

Process:

Have each child follow these steps to use the crumpling process:

1. Think of a floral design or scene you'd like to create. (If desired, first make a simple sketch on a sheet of construction paper.)
2. Crumple select colors of tissue paper into small wads.
3. Glue each tissue paper wad to the construction paper to create or fill in your design.
4. Set your project aside to dry.

Finishing Touches

Invite each child to trim around her completed design. Then have her crumple additional tissue squares and glue them atop the already glued tissue wads on her project. You'll find that the result soars to new heights!

Crumpling

Crumpled Crayon Crackle

Take crayon drawings from interesting to extraordinary with this technique!

Materials:
- class supply of art paper
- crayons
- deep bowl of diluted black tempera paint

Setup:
Arrange the materials for easy student access.

Process:
Have each child follow these steps to use the crumpling process:

1. Decide on a simple design you'd like to color.
2. Color the design on a sheet of art paper. Apply the crayon heavily and fill in as much area with crayon as possible.
3. Crumple the completed picture into a small ball.
4. Dunk the ball into the diluted paint.
5. After a thorough soaking, remove the paper ball from the water.
6. Flatten the picture on a tabletop.
7. Hang the paper to dry overnight.

Finishing Touches

Heighten the effect of this technique by inviting each child to mount her picture on a sheet of black construction paper. What a standout result!

Cutting

Simple As a Straight Line

These abstract yet straightforward designs are just right for little hands!

Materials:
- black construction paper
- scissors
- white poster board squares in a variety of sizes
- glue

Setup:

Arrange the materials for easy student access.

Process:

Have each child follow these steps to use the cutting process:

1. Use scissors to cut strips of black paper.
2. Arrange the strips on your poster board square to make a design. When you like the way it looks, glue the strips down.
3. Cut, arrange, and glue more strips if desired.

Finishing Touches

For more fun, emphasize the spaces created from gluing the cut paper to the poster board. Invite each child to use markers to color some of the spaces. Who knew a simple straight line could be so cool?

Cutting

A Cut Above
Creative cutting leads to crisp collages!

Materials:
- colorful construction paper
- decorative-edge scissors
- school scissors
- white construction paper
- glue

Setup:
Arrange the materials for easy student access.

Process:
Have each child follow these steps to use the cutting process:
1. Use scissors to cut shapes from colorful construction paper. Try different kinds of scissors.
2. Glue your favorite shapes to a sheet of white paper. Overlap them if you like.
3. Cut and glue more shapes if desired.

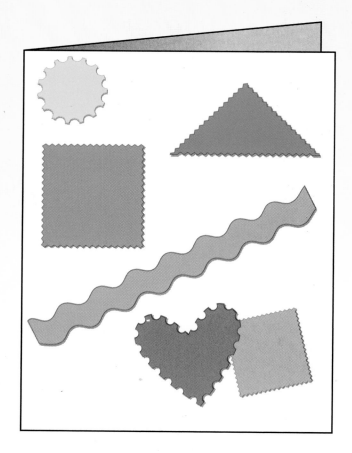

Finishing Touches

These collages can easily be made into greeting cards for loved ones. Simply have each child fold his dried collage in half. Write "I think you're a cut above the rest!" on the inside left of the card and invite him to write his name on the inside right. Encourage each child to give his card to someone special. Sweet!

Snip, Snip, Snowflakes!

Even the youngest students will have success in cutting these giant snowflake look-alikes!

Materials:
- class supply of paper doilies
- scissors

Setup:

Arrange the materials for easy student access.

Process:

Have each child follow these steps to use the cutting process:

1. Look at your doily and think about snowflakes.
2. Fold your doily in half; then fold it in half again.
3. Use scissors to cut shapes from your doily.
4. Unfold and enjoy the snowflake!

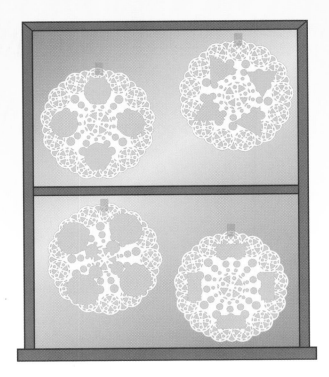

Finishing Touches

For a blizzardlike display, tape each child's snowflake to a window. Brrr—looks like snow!

Dipping

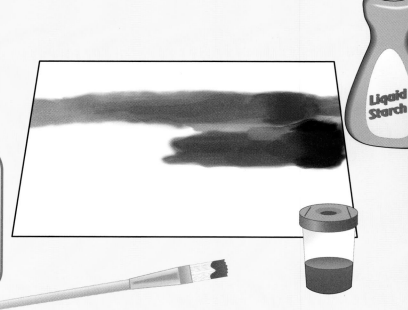

Magic Paint

What happens when you wet paper with liquid starch and then dab on paint? You get a soft, magical effect that washes over the paper!

Materials:
- class supply of white construction paper
- container of liquid starch
- small containers of tempera paint
- paintbrushes

Setup:
Arrange the materials for easy student access.

Process:
Have each child follow these steps to use the dipping process:
1. Paint your whole paper with liquid starch and leave it wet.
2. Dip a paintbrush into one color of paint and dab it onto your paper.
3. Swish the paint across your paper to create long streaks of color. Watch how the streaks change and react to the wet starch on your paper.
4. Repeat the process with additional colors of paint.
5. Set your paper aside to dry.

Finishing Touches

Mount each child's creation on a larger sheet of colored construction paper and display it on a bulletin board titled "Dabbling in Paint." For added learning, invite each child to write (or dictate) a word describing the process or resulting project on an index card. Attach the cards to the display and read them together. Swirly! Striped! Feathery!

Dip and Dye

This simple technique will leave your youngsters fit to be "dyed"!

Materials:
- class supply of white paper towels
- food coloring
- water

Setup:
1. Pour several drops of each color of food coloring into a separate small container. Slightly dilute each with water to make dye.
2. Arrange the prepared dyes and paper towels for easy student access.

Process:
Have each child follow these steps to use the dipping process:
1. Fold your paper towel several times to make a small square.
2. Hold your square firmly and then dip one corner of it into one container of dye.
3. Repeat Step 2 by dipping each remaining corner of your square into a different color of dye.
4. Unfold your paper towel and lay it flat to dry.

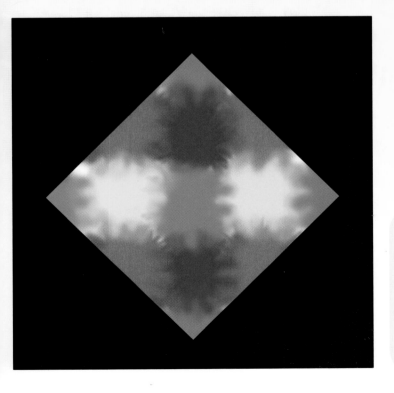

Finishing Touches

Invite each child to create a fun frame to show off her dip-and-dye project! Have her fold a piece of construction paper in half. Then help her draw a shape on the fold of the paper and cut it out. Have each child unfold her paper frame and glue her dyed towel to the back. Let the glue dry; then trim any excess towel from around the frame. Groovy!

Dipping

String Them Along

Dip into this paint process for some colorful fun!

Materials:
- class supply of white construction paper
- 1' lengths of yarn (one for each different color of paint)
- spring-type clothespins (one for each different color of paint)
- shallow containers of water-thinned liquid tempera paint

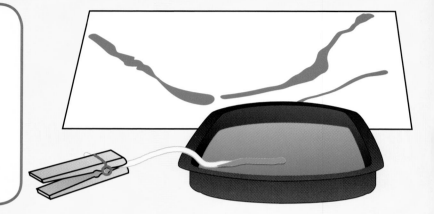

Setup:
1. Attach a clothespin to one end of each piece of yarn to form a handle.
2. Arrange the prepared paints and yarns for easy student access.

Process:

Have each child follow these steps to use the dipping process:
1. Hold a piece of yarn by the clothespin handle. Dip the yarn into one color of paint. Then hold the yarn up over the paint container to allow the excess paint to drip off.
2. Lay the yarn on your sheet of paper and drag it across to make a swirl of color.
3. Put the clothespin and yarn next to the container with the matching color of paint.
4. Choose another color of paint. Repeat Steps 1–3 with different colors of paint.

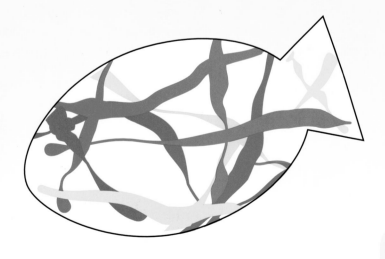

Finishing Touches

Youngsters will get hooked on transforming their string art into these beautiful fish! Help each child draw a simple fish shape onto her string art project and then cut it out. Tape the fish to your classroom windows for an aquarium effect. Pretty!

Dripping

Trickle Tint

Drip, drop! Youngsters are sure to enjoy creating colorful shapes with this no-mess method.

Materials:
- Pellon fabric (available at fabric stores)
- food coloring
- eyedroppers
- pie pans
- water-filled spray bottle
- small containers of water
- scissors

Setup:
1. Cut a class supply of geometric shapes from Pellon fabric.
2. Tint each container of water a different color by adding drops of food coloring until the desired shade is reached.
3. Arrange the remaining materials for easy student access.

Process:
Have each child follow these steps to use the dripping process:
1. Choose a shape; then use the spray bottle to mist it with water. Place your shape in a pie pan.
2. Use an eyedropper to drip one color of tinted water onto the shape. Repeat the process with different colors as desired.
3. Remove your shape from the pan and set it aside to dry.

Finishing Touches

Why not display youngsters' completed shapes on your flannelboard to enhance your lessons? Pellon fabric is durable, easily sticks to your flannelboard, and holds color very well. It's hip to be square!

Dripping

Split, Splat!

Stocking up on simple dripping techniques? Try this one on for size!

Materials:
- several pairs of panty hose (one leg for each color of paint)
- sand
- bowls of thinned tempera paint
- class supply of 12" x 18" white construction paper

Setup:
1. Cut the legs off of each pair of panty hose. Fill the toe of each leg with approximately two cups of sand. Then tie each leg above the sand to form a ball and tail as shown.
2. Arrange the prepared hose and paint for easy student access.

Process:
Have each child follow these steps to use the dripping process:
1. Holding the tail, dip one ball into a bowl of paint. Let the excess paint drip off into the bowl.
2. Stand over your paper. Hold the tail so that the ball is over your paper and then drop the ball.
3. Using a clean sand ball for each color of paint, repeat the process as you like.
4. Set your paper aside to dry.

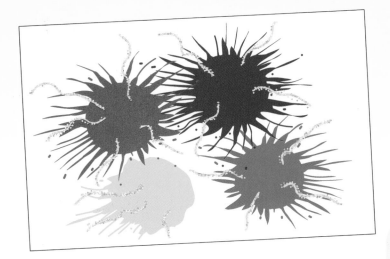

Finishing Touches

Create shimmery bursts of color by having youngsters add streaks of glitter glue to each paint splatter. Use youngsters' creations as a fireworks display on a bulletin board. Now "hose" about that for a fun project?

Superb Stains

This technique creates an ink stain that youngsters will be praised for producing!

Materials:
- class supply of thin (uncoated) white paper plates
- class supply of coffee filters
- washable markers
- eyedroppers
- small containers of water
- masking tape

Setup:

Arrange the materials for easy student access.

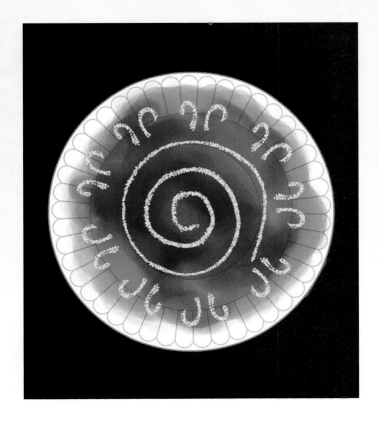

Process:

Have each child follow these steps to use the dripping process:

1. Flatten your coffee filter and lay it on top of your paper plate. Use small pieces of tape to attach the edges of the filter to the plate.
2. Color the filter with markers (blue and green produce especially good effects).
3. Use an eyedropper to drip water over the filter, making the ink spread into unique designs.
4. Remove the filter to see the design left behind on the plate.
5. Set the plate aside to dry.

Finishing Touches

For a display that's out of this world, have each child pretend his designed plate is a planet. Invite him to add glitter glue to create sparkling effects; then mount the resulting projects on a bulletin board covered with black paper. Cosmic!

Air Painting

Dazzle your little ones with this technique, which won't leave brushstrokes behind!

Materials:
- class supply of construction paper
- thinned tempera paint
- paintbrushes

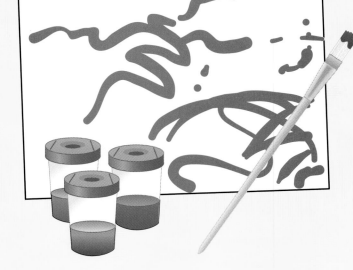

Setup:

Arrange the materials for easy student access.

Process:

Have each child follow these steps to use the drizzling process:

1. Think about different kinds of lines, such as straight, curved, squiggly, and wavy.
2. Choose a color of paint. Dip a paintbrush into it.
3. Hold the paintbrush over your paper and move it in lines so that the paint drizzles onto your paper.
4. Repeat Steps 2 and 3 with different colors and types of lines.
5. Set your paper aside to dry.

Finishing Touches

Consider transforming these drizzle paintings into colorful creatures! Invite each child to think of brightly colored animals, such as birds, butterflies, fish, or insects. Then help her draw and cut out an appropriate shape from her painting. Suspend these colorful creatures from your classroom ceiling for a cheerful display. Just gorgeous!

Drizzling

Sweetheart Art

These shiny hearts are one of a kind!

Materials:
- class supply of craft foam heart cutouts
- squeeze bottles (one for each color of syrup)
- corn syrup
- food coloring
- glitter

Setup:
1. Pour corn syrup into the squeeze bottles. Add a few drops of food coloring to tint each portion a different color. Stir well.
2. Arrange the heart cutouts and prepared squeeze bottles for easy student access.

Process:

Have each child follow these steps to use the drizzling process:
1. Choose a color of syrup. Squeeze the bottle to drizzle some onto your heart cutout.
2. Drizzle different colors of syrup onto your cutout.
3. Sprinkle glitter over the wet syrup.
4. Set your cutout aside to dry for three to four days.

Finishing Touches

Since home is where the heart is, why not make these shiny hearts into door hangers? Simply punch a hole in each heart and tie on a ribbon hanger. On the back of the heart, write "Home is where the heart is!" Below the phrase, have each child write his name or initials.

Drizzling

Stuck on Art
Here's a fun idea you can really cling to!

Materials:
- class supply of 8-inch waxed paper squares
- several bottles of white glue
- food coloring

Setup:
1. Add a few drops of food coloring to tint each bottle of glue a different color. Stir well.
2. Arrange the waxed paper and prepared glue bottles for easy student access.

Process:
Have each child follow these steps to use the drizzling process:
1. Choose a color of glue. Squeeze the bottle to drizzle some onto your waxed paper.
2. Drizzle different colors of glue onto your paper to make a design. It's okay to use a lot of glue!
3. Set your design aside to dry for two to three days.
4. When the glue is completely dry, peel away the waxed paper.

Finishing Touches
These designs really shine, so why not stick a few to your windows? They'll cling to glass without any additional adhesive. If desired, also suspend a few from your classroom ceiling with yarn. Your youngsters are sure to love the way these drizzle designs catch the light!

 # Fingerpainting

Glistening Shapes

Break away from the ordinary. Consider this glistening fingerpaint option!

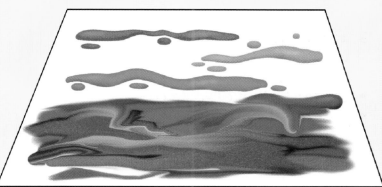

Materials:
- class supply of construction paper cutouts (any shape)
- sweetened condensed milk
- food coloring

Setup:
1. Make milk paint by mixing sweetened condensed milk and food coloring. Repeat to make batches in several colors.
2. Arrange the materials for easy student access.

Process:
Have each child follow these steps to use the fingerpainting process:
1. Select a cutout.
2. Fingerpaint your cutout using milk paint. Use several colors for an interesting blend.
3. Set aside your fingerpainting to dry overnight.

Finishing Touches

The glistening effect of this paint is dazzling, especially with extra lighting. Consider adding a string of white indoor holiday lights to surround a display of these paintings. The extra lighting will add to the glamour! Ta-da!

Fingerpainting

Puffy Painting

This fabulous textured paint adds lots of sensory appeal to this project!

Materials:
- class supply of tagboard cutouts (any shape)
- washable tempera paint
- white glue
- nonmentholated shaving cream
- glitter

Setup:
1. Mix several different colors of puff paint by combining two tablespoons of tempera paint and $\frac{1}{3}$ cup of white glue. Then fold in two cups of shaving cream until the color is well blended. Repeat with different paint colors. (Use the mixture shortly after creating it.)
2. Arrange the materials for easy student access.

Process:
Have each child follow these steps to use the fingerpainting process:
1. Select a tagboard cutout.
2. Using several colors of puff paint, fingerpaint unique designs on your cutout.
3. Sprinkle glitter over the wet paint.
4. Set your painting aside to dry overnight.

Finishing Touches

To elaborate on this appealing texture, encourage students to close their eyes and touch their completed paintings. Ask each child to use descriptive words to tell a buddy about her painting based only on the senses of touch and smell. Sensational!

Fingerpainting

Surf, Sun, and Sugar Paint

Sweet paint and fancy fingerpainting lead to a unique surfside display.

Materials:
- class supply of construction paper cutouts (a mixture of starfish, fish, shells, suns, or other ocean or beach shapes)
- crayons
- sugar
- food coloring
- water

Setup:
1. Mix a batch of sugar paint by combining sugar and several drops of food coloring with enough water to create a thick but paintable mixture. Repeat with an assortment of colors.
2. Arrange the materials for easy student access.

Process:
Have each child follow these steps to use the fingerpainting process:
1. Choose a cutout for your project.
2. Fingerpaint your cutout using sugar paint.
3. Set your fingerpainting aside to dry overnight.

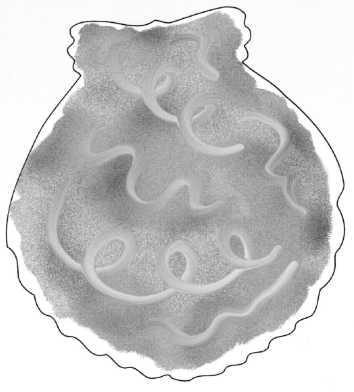

Finishing Touches

Consider creating a sand and surf backdrop on a bulletin board to display these sensational seaside creations! What a swell way to show off works of art!

olding

Pretty Prints

Folding adds flair to this fun printing project.

Materials:
- class supply of coffee filters
- scissors
- 2 sheets of white copy paper per child
- shallow pans of diluted food coloring

Setup:

Arrange the materials for easy student access.

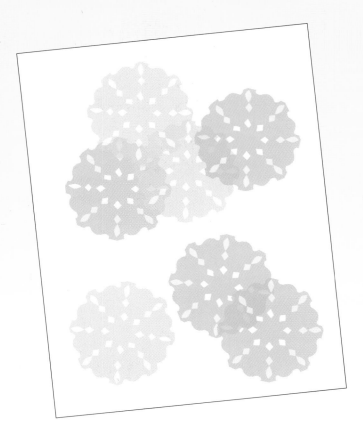

Process:

Have each child follow these steps to use the folding process:

1. Fold your coffee filter several times.
2. Snip and cut to create an interesting shape from the folded filter.
3. Unfold the filter shape and place it in a pan of food coloring.
4. Remove the filter shape from the pan after a desired amount of food coloring has been absorbed.
5. Place the filter shape onto a sheet of white paper.
6. Cover it with another sheet of white paper and press the sheets together.
7. Gently peel the sheets apart to reveal the designs.
8. Repeat Steps 3–7 several times with darker colors (to prevent muddying).
9. Set your papers aside to dry.

Finishing Touches

Consider inviting each child to use his artwork as decorative stationery. Have each student cut his papers into quarters for notecards. If desired, use the folding technique to decorate envelopes as well as paper.

Folding

Folding Flaps

Your youngsters will be the hit of the school when they show off these impressive paintings featuring a fold-and-press technique.

Materials:
- class supply of white paper squares
- tempera paint in squeeze bottles

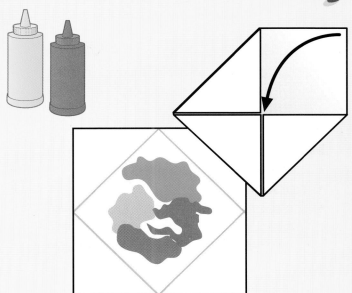

Setup:

Arrange the materials for easy student access.

Process:

Have each child follow these steps to use the folding process:

1. Place a paper square in front of you and locate the middle.
2. Fold each corner to the center of your paper square.
3. Unfold the paper and notice the inner square that is formed by the creases.
4. Select several paint colors and lightly squirt paint designs on the inner square.
5. Carefully press each corner inward to cover the paint.
6. Peel back each corner to see the finished painting.
7. Set the project aside to dry overnight.

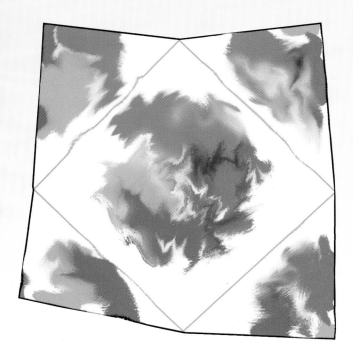

Finishing Touches

For an interesting display, attach the finished paintings to a bulletin board by the inner square only, allowing the corners to bend out slightly. This added dimension creates a special effect. Mesmerizing!

Folding

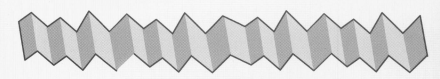

Fold-and-Cut Flowers

A basic accordion fold takes on a new shape with this clever idea!

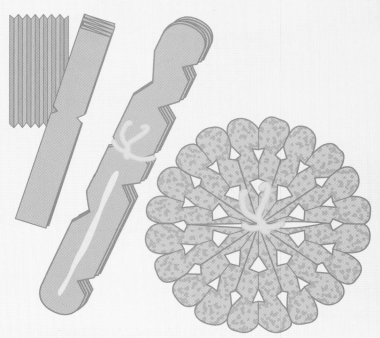

Materials:
- class supply of colored copy paper
- scissors
- class supply of pipe cleaners cut to 6" lengths
- glue

Setup:
Arrange the materials for easy student access.

Process:
Have each child follow these steps to use the folding process:

1. Beginning with a short side, accordion-fold your paper using one-inch folds.
   (For each child, cut a notch on each long side in the center of the folded paper as shown.)
2. Twist a pipe cleaner around the notches. Leave the two ends exposed to create the flower's stamen.
3. Make a variety of cuts on all sides of the folded paper.
4. Run a line of glue along one outside pleat.
5. Pull the flower open to attach it to the opposite outside pleat.
6. Repeat Steps 4 and 5 to attach the other side of the flower. *(Note: The completed flower will round in slightly like a bowl.)*

Finishing Touches

To vary the look, invite each child to apply a painting technique, such as splattering or sponging, to the paper and allow it to dry prior to beginning the project. If desired, mount the finished flowers on a bulletin board titled "Fancy Flowers."

Prehistoric Prints

Stomp! Stomp! Your little ones will romp through this process!

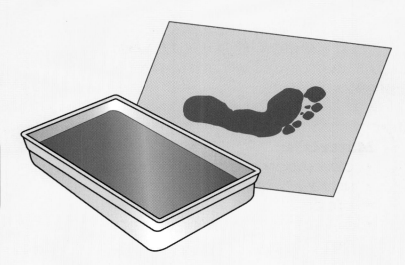

Materials:
- class supply of construction paper
- shallow containers of washable tempera paint

Setup:

Arrange the materials for easy student access.

Process:

Have each child follow these steps to use the printing process:

1. Choose a color of paint. Carefully place the sole of one foot in the paint.
2. Step onto your paper to make a footprint or two.
3. Set your paper aside to dry.

Kirkceratops

Finishing Touches

When the paint is dry, invite each child to use crayons, markers, paper scraps, and glue to transform his print into a prehistoric creature. When the artist is through, help him name his creature, somehow incorporating his own name. Display the projects and read all the made-up names as a class. Now that's printing made "dino-mite"!

Printing

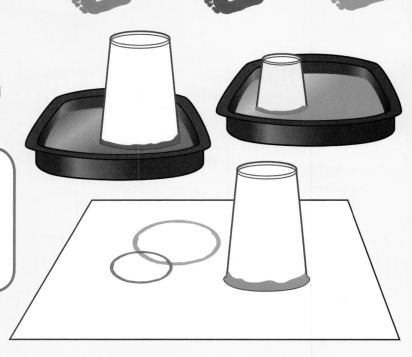

Paper Cup Printing

Focus on circles with this well-rounded printing process!

Materials:
- class supply of construction paper
- shallow containers of tempera paint
- several different sizes of paper cups

Setup:
Arrange the materials for easy student access.

Process:
Have each child follow these steps to use the printing process:

1. Look at the different sizes of cups and notice the size of the circle each can make.
2. Choose a color of paint. Dip the rim of a paper cup into it.
3. Print the cup rim on your paper.
4. Repeat Steps 2 and 3 with different colors and sizes of circles. Overlap the circles if you like.
5. Set your paper aside to dry.

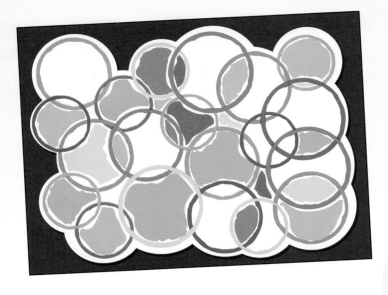

Finishing Touches

When the paint is dry, invite each child to use crayons or markers to color areas created by overlapping the circles. Then help him cut around the perimeter of his design and glue it to a sheet of black construction paper for a dazzling work of art!

Printing

Bubble Wrap Fun

Who knew packing material could create such interesting prints? Try it!

Materials:
- assorted shapes cut from bubble wrap
- class supply of construction paper
- shallow containers of washable tempera paint

Setup:

Arrange the materials for easy student access.

Process:

Have each child follow these steps to use the printing process:
1. Choose a shape and a color of paint. Dip the shape, bubble side down, into the paint.
2. Print the shape on your paper.
3. Repeat Steps 1 and 2 as you like.
4. Set your paper aside to dry.

Finishing Touches

When the paint is dry, invite each child to use crayons or markers to add details to her picture or design. For a twist, try this activity with seasonal or thematic shapes. How festive!

Rolling

Simply Stripes!

This easy rolling activity quickly adds stripes to any paper project.

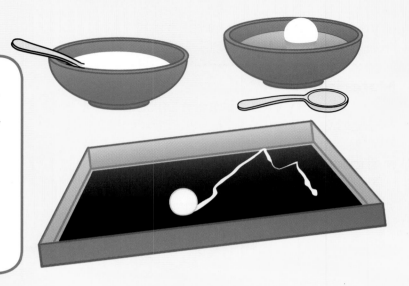

Materials:
- class supply of art paper or precut paper shapes (seasonal, thematic, etc.)
- small bowls of tempera paint in a variety of colors
- spoons
- box lid or plastic container
- Ping-Pong balls, paddleballs, or golf balls

Setup:
1. Place a spoon and a ball in each paint bowl. (You can use an assortment of ball types or all the same kind.)
2. Arrange the materials for easy student access.

Process:
Have each child follow these steps to use the rolling process:
1. Select a piece of paper or a paper cutout.
2. Place the paper faceup in the bottom of the lid (or container).
3. Use the spoon to scoop out the ball from a desired color of paint.
4. Gently place the ball on top of your paper.
5. Tilt the lid (or container) back and forth allowing the ball to roll painted lines across your paper in a variety of directions.
6. If desired, replace the ball with a different paint-covered ball to make multicolored stripes.

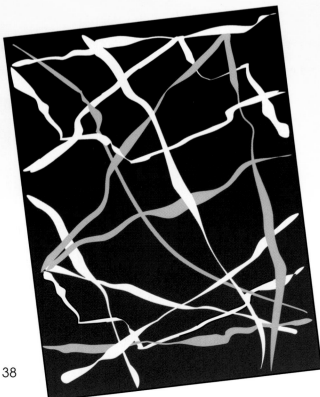

Finishing Touches

Create a dramatic reverse effect by featuring dark art paper and white, yellow, or neon-colored paints. Encourage students to try the various materials. Wow, those are some sassy stripes!

Rolling

Totally Tubular Paintings!

Lots of different items can be used to create these unique rolled paintings.

Materials:
- class supply of art paper
- shallow pans of tempera paint in a variety of colors
- tube-shaped textured tool (a round plastic hairbrush, an ear of sweet corn without leaves, etc.)

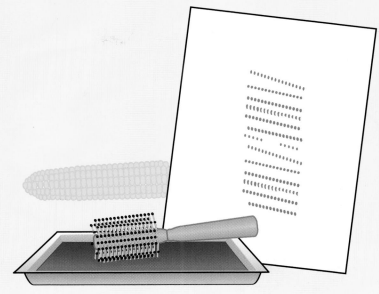

Setup:
1. Decide on the number of colors you want to use and provide a textured tool for each color. (This will avoid needing to rinse off the item between uses.)
2. Arrange the materials for easy student access.

Process:
Have each child follow these steps to use the rolling process:
1. Decide which paint and textured tool you want to use.
2. Roll the tool in paint.
3. Roll the tool on your paper.
4. Repeat steps 2 and 3 as needed to cover the paper.

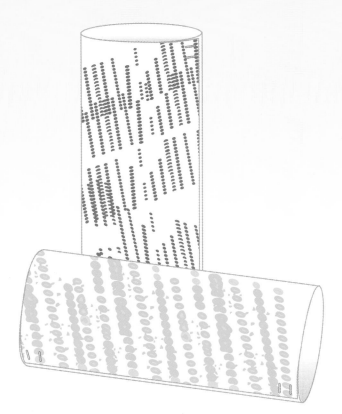

Finishing Touches

For a unique display that mimics the tools used in the technique, roll the paper, art side out, to make a tube and then secure the edge where the ends meet. Stand these finished masterpieces for a totally tubular display.

Rolling

Tornado Technique

When this whirlwind painting technique storms your classroom, the aftermath is a rainbow of beautiful art!

Materials:
- class supply of art paper cut into 7½" x 11" sheets
- plastic two-liter bottles with lids attached
- X-acto knife
- marbles (one for each bottle)
- plastic wrap
- rubber bands
- tempera paint in a variety of colors
- plastic spoons (one for each color of paint)

Setup:
1. In advance, create a tornado painter for each color of paint you desire. To make one, cut the bottom off a two-liter bottle and prepare a double layer of plastic wrap that will thoroughly cover the cut end. Place a marble in the bottle and a rubber band nearby.
2. Arrange the paint and paper for easy student access.

Process:
Have each child follow these steps to use the rolling process:
1. Line the inside of a tornado painter with a sheet of art paper.
2. Use a spoon to add three or four drops of paint.
3. Cover the open end of the painter with two layers of plastic wrap and secure the wrap with a rubber band.
4. Tilt the bottle to move the marble out of the neck and then rotate the painter with a tornado motion.
5. Remove the paper and place it in a different painter to add additional color.

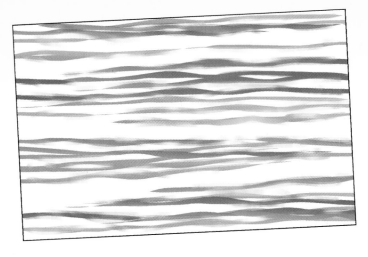

Finishing Touches

For a lasting display, cover a bulletin board with side-by-side tornado paintings. Then use that colorful backdrop to display other completed student work. Neat!

Rubbing

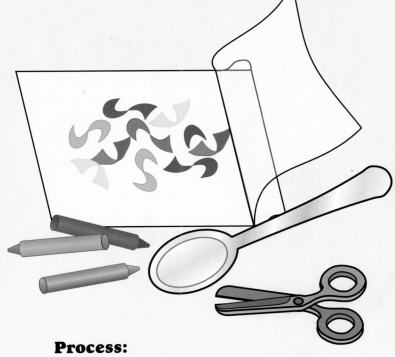

Cool Color Rub!

This variation of the popular crayon-melt idea will rub you the *right* way!

Materials:

- class supply of clear self-adhesive paper sheets
- crayon shavings
- large metal spoon
- tape (optional)

Setup:

Arrange the materials for easy student access.

Process:

Have each child follow these steps to use the rubbing process:

1. Lay your adhesive sheet with the sticky side up on a table. *(Tape the corners down if they curl up.)*
2. Cover half of the adhesive with colorful crayon shavings.
3. Fold the other half over the shavings.
4. Rub over the adhesive, pressing hard, with the back of a large metal spoon. Make sure to rub until all the adhesive is stuck together.

Finishing Touches

Hanging the results of this process in a window adds to the appeal! If desired, have each child cut his resulting project into a shape using a template. Punch a hole; then thread and tie a piece of yarn for hanging. Now that's a first-rate rubbing!

Rubbing

Masking Tape Magic

Youngsters will be delighted with the magical results of this rubbing process.

Materials:
- class supply of art paper
- masking tape
- crayons with the paper removed

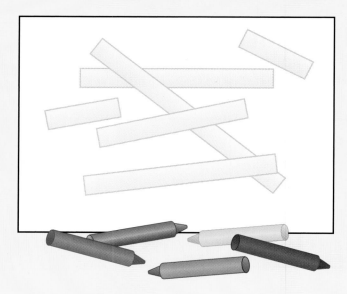

Setup:

Arrange the materials for easy student access.

Process:

Have each child follow these steps to use the rubbing process:

1. In random places, attach several strips of masking tape to your sheet of art paper. Overlap some for an interesting effect.
2. Using the edge of a crayon, make bold strokes of color across the enhanced paper.

Finishing Touches

Turn up the interest on this by inviting each child to use a number of different colors while rubbing. For another varied look, supply different colors of masking tape too!

Clay Another Way

Turn your students' imaginations loose with this interesting approach to working with clay.

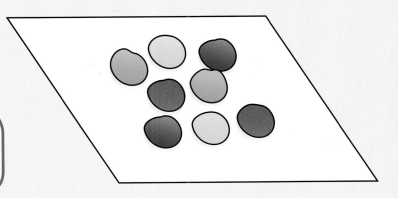

Materials:
- several colors of clay
- class supply of 6" x 6" art paper

Setup:
Arrange the materials for easy student access.

Process:
Have each child follow these steps to use the rubbing process:
1. Select small amounts of several colors of clay.
2. Put small dabs of the clay onto your art paper.
3. Press and rub the clay to stretch it several directions. Keep pressing and rubbing to slightly blend the colors together.

Finishing Touches

Help each child trim around her finished rubbing to create a unique leaf shape. Display the shapes in your classroom to bring the artistic outdoors inside!

Spaghetti Sculpture

This hands-on technique turns oodles of noodles into air-dried art.

Materials:
- cooked and rinsed spaghetti noodles
- plastic bowls
- white glue
- food coloring
- 9" x 12" sheet of waxed paper
- 9" x 12" sheet of tagboard
- glue

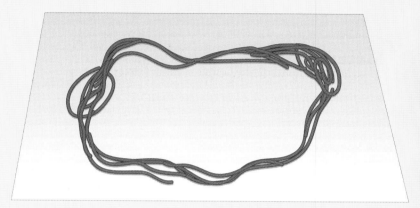

Setup:
1. In a plastic bowl, mix a small amount of white glue with any color of food coloring until the desired shade is reached. Add an amount of cooked noodles and toss to coat. Repeat with other colors to tint a class supply of noodles.
2. Arrange the colored noodles and waxed paper for easy student access.

Process:
Have each child follow these steps to use the shaping process:
1. Decide what color noodles you want to use.
2. Shape and mold the spaghetti atop the waxed paper to make a sculpture. Experiment with height, width, and texture.
3. Let the sculpture air-dry for two to three days.
4. Carefully remove the dried sculpture from the waxed paper.
5. Glue your spaghetti sculpture onto the colored tagboard.

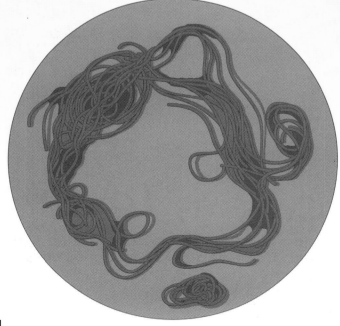

Finishing Touches

Host a gallery opening! Display the finished projects on tabletops for students to view and compare. If desired, invite school personnel to tour the gallery and discuss the exhibits with your little sculptors. Fabulous!

Shaping and Molding

Awesome Animals

Just a handful of cereal adds interesting texture to this traditional molding technique.

Materials:
- assorted animal pictures (optional)
- Crayola Model Magic modeling compound
- cereal rings or other cereal shapes
- craft glue
- markers

Setup:

Arrange the materials for easy student access.

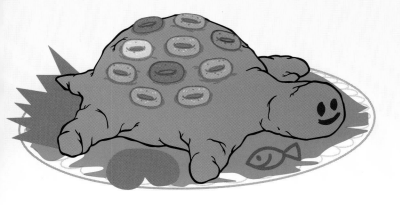

Process:

Have each child follow these steps to use the shaping and molding process:

1. Think about animals with interesting body coverings, such as turtles, snakes, and fish. Look at pictures to help you plan the type of animal you'd like to make.
2. Shape and mold a handful of modeling compound into your desired animal shape.
3. Press cereal shapes into your sculpture to add texture. Use dabs of craft glue to secure the cereal.
4. Set aside your animal sculpture to dry overnight.
5. Use markers to add details.

Finishing Touches

Why not have each child create a miniature habitat for her animal sculpture? Provide paper scraps, markers, leftover cereal, and glue for each child to use to create a simple scene on a small paper plate. Help her glue her sculpture to its habitat and then display as desired. Awesome!

Shaping and Molding

"Yarn-tastic" Masterpieces

Try this yarn-shaping technique any time of year!

Materials:
- class supply of tagboard squares in a variety of sizes
- 12-inch lengths of colorful yarn
- glue

Setup:

1. Sketch a simple seasonal or thematic shape onto a square of tagboard for each child.
2. Arrange the materials for easy student access.

Process:

Have each child follow these steps to use the shaping and molding process:

1. Choose a shape and decide what colors of yarn you want to use to fill it in.
2. Spread glue on the shape.
3. Coil and press lengths of yarn into the glue, molding it to fit the shape.
4. If desired, fill in the background with the same method.

Finishing Touches

If desired, display the finished designs in the style of a quilt on a bulletin board. Add the title "An Impressive Patchwork."

Sponging

Masking Tape Suprise!

This easy sponging process is perfect for your pint-size Picassos!

Materials:
- class supply of fingerpaint paper
- strips of masking tape in various sizes
- shallow containers of tempera paint
- damp sponges in various sizes (one for each color of paint)

Setup:
Arrange the materials for easy student access.

Process:
Have each child follow these steps to use the sponging process:
1. Arrange a few strips of masking tape on your paper. Overlap the pieces if you like.
2. Use a sponge to press paint on your paper.
3. Sponge-paint with different colors until all the tape is covered.
4. When the paint is almost dry, carefully peel off the tape.
5. Set your paper aside to dry.

Finishing Touches

If desired, encourage each child to make a design with his tape pieces. Then have him complete the process as described above. Laminate the resulting projects for great book and journal covers. "Write" on!

Sponging

Fun Foliage
These colorful leaves are just lovely!

Materials:
- brown paper grocery bags
- shallow containers of tempera paint in various shades of green and yellow
- damp sponges in various sizes (one for each color of paint)

Setup:
1. Cut down one side of each bag and remove the bottom. Thoroughly wet each bag and then crumple it. Spread the bags flat to dry. From the bags, cut two large leaf shapes for each child.
2. Arrange the remaining materials for easy student access.

Process:
Have each child follow these steps to use the sponging process:
1. Use a sponge to press paint onto your leaf cutout.
2. Sponge-paint with another color until the leaf is covered.
3. Repeat with your other leaf cutout, but be sure to use different shades of green.
4. Set your leaves aside to dry.

Finishing Touches
For a seasonal display, arrange the leaves as a bulletin board border. Or mount a supply on a wall to resemble a large wreath. If desired, glue an arrangement of leaves to a cardboard ring to make a door-size wreath. You'll rake up piles of creative ways to display these leaves!

Sponge Designs

Combine the best parts of sponging and printing with this no-mess process!

Materials:
- class supply of construction paper
- tempera paint
- paintbrushes
- damp jumbo sponges
- container of water

Setup:
1. Arrange the materials for easy student access.
2. Help students rinse and wring out the sponges between printings.

Process:
Have each child follow these steps to use the sponging process:
1. Think about the kind of design you'd like to sponge.
2. Paint your design onto the sponge.
3. Press the sponge, painted side down, onto your paper. Carefully pick it up and look at your design.
4. Rinse and wring out your sponge; then repeat Steps 2–4 if you want to.
5. Set your sponge-printing aside to dry.

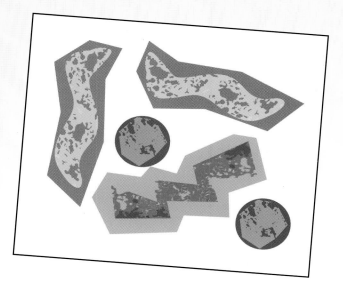

Finishing Touches

Invite each child to trim around her sponge prints and glue them onto a sheet of colorful construction paper to create a collage. Wow, you made that with a sponge? Cool!

eading

oth Moves!

Here ... ly sensational activity that will spread a little fun!

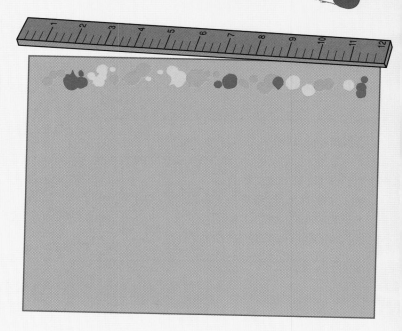

Materials:
- class supply of construction paper
- small containers of tempera paint
- plastic spoons (one per container)
- class supply of plastic rulers

Setup:
1. Put a spoon into each container of tempera paint.
2. Arrange the materials for easy student access.

Process:
Have each child follow these steps to use the spreading process:
1. Choose up to three colors of paint. Use the spoon to drip a few drops of each color near the top of your paper.
2. Spread the paint by dragging a ruler downward from the top of the paper. Zigzag the ruler a little as you work downward.
3. Set your paper aside to dry.

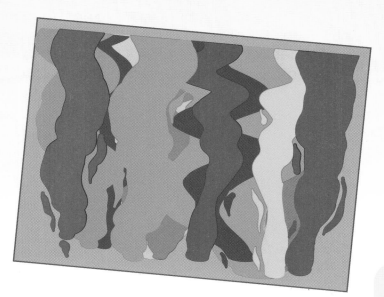

Finishing Touches

Invite each child to use this colorful paper for journal covers, gift wrap, book covers, and more! Spread some cool colors throughout your school day!

Spreading

Here's the Scoop

I scream; you scream; we'll all scream for a cool technique that smacks of summer!

Materials:
- class supply of construction paper
- crayons
- nonmentholated shaving cream
- white glue
- class supply of craft sticks
- multicolored glitter

Setup:

1. Make ice-cream paint by briskly folding two parts of nonmentholated shaving cream with one part of white glue. Add food coloring if desired. Fold the mixture until it is slightly stiff and shiny. (Two cups of shaving cream and one cup of glue yield enough ice-cream paint for approximately 14 portions.)
2. Arrange the materials for easy student access.

Process:

Have each child follow these steps to use the spreading process:

1. Draw and color an ice-cream cone or dish on your paper.
2. Drop a dollop of ice-cream paint onto your paper above your drawing.
3. Spread the paint with a craft stick until it resembles a scoop of ice cream.
4. Shake on a few glitter sprinkles.
5. Set your paper aside to dry overnight.

Finishing Touches

The projects that result from this spreading technique are just perfect for an end-of-the-year display! Mount each child's ice-cream picture with a special photo from the school year. Title the display "We've Had a 'Scooper-Duper' Year!"

Spreading

Firecracker, Firecracker!

Boom, boom, boom! These dazzling fireworks explode with color and sparkle!

Materials:
- class supply of black construction paper
- bowls of thick tempera paint
- ultrafine glitter
- plastic spoons
- cotton swabs

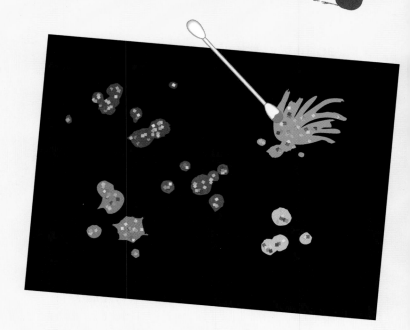

Setup:
1. Mix some glitter into each color of paint.
2. Arrange the materials for easy student access.

Process:

Have each child follow these steps to use the spreading process:
1. Use a spoon to put a few drops of each color of paint onto your paper.
2. Using a different cotton swab for each color, spread the paint away from the drops until they resemble fireworks.
3. Shake on more glitter.
4. Set your paper aside to dry overnight.

Finishing Touches

For a big bang, cluster the finished fireworks on a bulletin board covered with black paper. Ooh! Aah!

Sprinkling

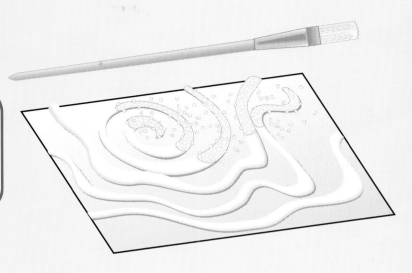

Salty Squiggles

Looking for interesting texture from common materials? This process guarantees it!

Materials:
- class supply of card stock squares in a variety of sizes
- glue
- salt

Setup:
Arrange the materials for easy student access.

Process:
Have each child follow these steps to use the sprinkling process:

1. Think about a design you'd like to make on your card stock square.
2. Squirt glue onto the card stock to make the design.
3. While the glue is wet, pour on salt to completely cover the glue. Shake off the excess.
4. Repeat Steps 2 and 3 until your card stock is covered with a cool design.
5. Set your paper aside to dry overnight.

Finishing Touches

Add color to spice up these salty designs. Invite each child to dip a small paintbrush into the watercolor of her choice and then carefully touch it to her design. Have her watch as the color is immediately absorbed. Then encourage her to add more color where desired. Let the resulting project dry overnight; then shake off any loose salt. Don't forget to throw a little over your shoulder!

Sprinkling

Sparkly Sand Art

What do you get when you sprinkle sand on liquid starch? You get beautiful artwork!

Materials:
- class supply of corrugated cardboard squares in various sizes
- liquid starch
- paintbrushes
- sand
- glitter

Setup:

Arrange the materials for easy student access.

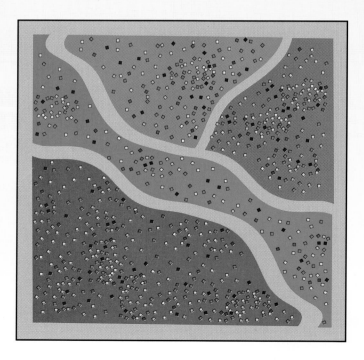

Process:

Have each child follow these steps to use the sprinkling process:

1. Think about a design you'd like to make on your cardboard square.
2. Paint liquid starch on one area of your square.
3. Sprinkle sand to completely cover the starch. Sprinkle glitter over the sand. Shake off the excess.
4. Repeat Steps 2 and 3 with different colors of glitter until your square is covered with a design.
5. Set your sand art aside to dry overnight.

Finishing Touches

The Native Americans of the Southwest and Plains are known for their sand art. If desired, share pictures of Navajo, Pueblo, Apache, Cheyenne, or Arapaho designs with students before they begin this process; then encourage them to create similar designs. You may wish to use colored sand instead of glitter to make students' designs look more authentic.

Marvelous Mosaics

This centuries-old process is made simple for little hands.

Materials:
- uncooked rice
- rubbing alcohol
- water
- food coloring
- paper towels
- plastic bowls
- class supply of tagboard shapes
- yarn precut into various lengths
- glue

Setup:
1. Tint several batches of rice by first mixing a small amount of rubbing alcohol and food coloring. Soak rice in this mixture until the desired shade is reached. Drain the rice on paper towels overnight; then put each color of rice in a separate bowl.
2. Arrange the prepared rice, tagboard shapes, yarn, and glue for easy student access.

Process:
Have each child follow these steps to use the sprinkling process:
1. Think about a design you'd like to make on your tagboard shape.
2. Glue on yarn to divide your shape into sections.
3. Spread glue in one area of your shape. Sprinkle rice to completely cover the glue. Shake off the excess.
4. Repeat Step 3 with different colors of rice until your shape is covered with a mosaic design.
5. Set your mosaic aside to dry overnight.

Finishing Touches

Why not add a seasonal flair to this colorful process? Simply make an assortment of tagboard shapes that correspond with an upcoming holiday or the current time of year. There are no limits!

...ue Paper Pictures

...oungsters have lots of room for creativity with this torn-tissue project!

Materials:
- several colors of tissue paper
- bowls of thinned white glue
- class supply of art paper
- paintbrush (for glue)

Setup:

Arrange the materials for easy student access.

Process:

Have each child follow these steps to use the tearing process:

1. Decide which colors of tissue paper you'd like to use for your project.
2. Tear a section of each tissue paper color into small pieces.
3. Coat the surface of the art paper with the thinned glue mixture.
4. Press the torn tissue paper pieces onto the glue, overlapping pieces as you work.
5. When your paper is completely covered, brush another layer of glue over the tissue paper.
6. Set the project aside to dry.

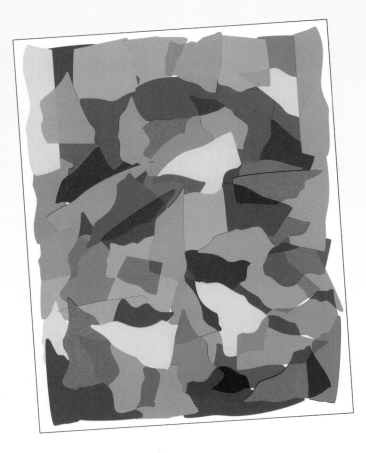

Finishing Touches

For a classy finish, coat each child's picture with a layer of glossy acrylic spray. (Apply outdoors and away from students.) Picasso or preschooler? Who will know?

Torn-Paper Animal Art

Your little ones will tear into this animal art!

Materials:
- several colors of construction paper
- glue

Setup:
1. Arrange the materials for easy student access.
2. If desired, share assorted animal pictures before having students begin their projects.

Process:

Have each child follow these steps to use the tearing process:
1. Decide what animal you'd like to create.
2. Tear construction paper to make the parts of the animal. Begin by tearing paper to make a body. Then tear more paper for a head, arms, legs, a tail, and so on as appropriate.
3. Glue the parts of the animal together.
4. Tear and glue additional details, such as eyes, teeth, or stripes.

Finishing Touches

Before beginning, you may want to determine a specific set of animals from a single habitat, such as a pond, an ocean, or a desert. When the torn-paper animals are complete, display them on a bulletin board backdrop created with the same torn-paper process. Onlookers will be awed by the imagination and energy that's reflected in this project!

Tearing

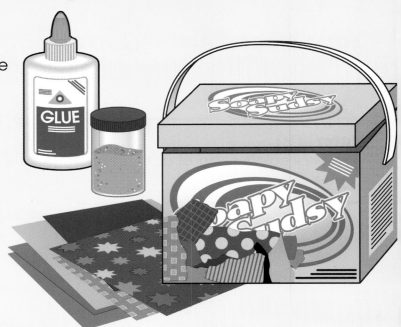

Treasured Totes

This tearing process results in a trinket tote sure to be treasured by your youngsters!

Materials:
- class supply of laundry detergent boxes with handles
- variety of paper (tissue paper, wallpaper, wrapping paper, construction paper, etc.)
- glue
- glitter

Setup:
Arrange the materials for easy student access.

Process:
Have each child follow these steps to use the tearing process:
1. Select a box and an assortment of paper.
2. Tear the paper into small pieces.
3. Glue the paper pieces to the outside of the box. Overlap the pieces and work to cover the box completely.
4. While the box is still damp with glue, sprinkle it with a coat of glitter. It will stick only in random places, but will be a dazzling addition!

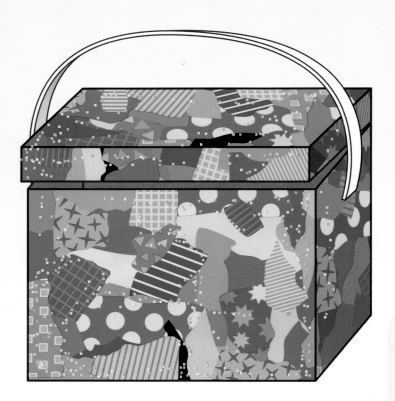

Finishing Touches

Consider having students store other completed art projects in these totes. When enough projects have been collected, host an art viewing. Provide table space for each child and have her unload her treasure tote to display her prized creations!

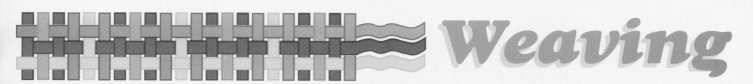

Weaving

Wondrous Weavings

Turn an average chain-link fence into a stunning work of art!

Materials:
- lengths of fabric scraps
- lengths of yarn
- lengths of ribbon
- lengths of twine
- access to a chain-link fence

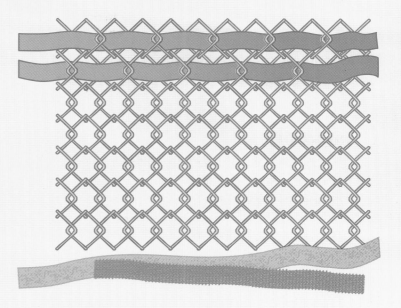

Setup:

Arrange the materials for easy student access.

Process:

Have each child follow these steps to use the weaving process:
1. Think about what kind of material you'd like to weave into the fence.
2. Weave your material, working it over and under the links. Try different kinds of material. Do they feel different? Is one type easier to weave than another?

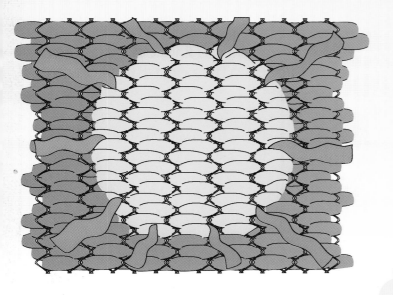

Finishing Touches

For a uniquely artistic display, encourage students to work together to plan a large design. Help them weave the body of the design with complementary materials. Then have students use other materials to weave in finishing touches. You'll have the best-dressed fence in town!

Weaving

Dazzling Dreamcatchers

Your little ones can weave this simplified version of a classic Native American craft.

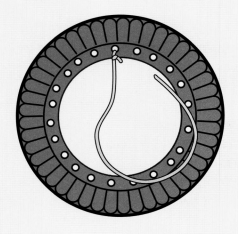

Materials:
- class supply of colored paper plates
- lengths of yarn
- access to scissors

Setup:
1. Cut the center out of each plate. Punch holes around the inside of the rims.
2. Arrange the materials for easy student access.

Process:
Have each child follow these steps to use the weaving process:
1. Tie one end of a length of yarn to a hole.
2. Weave the yarn by threading the yarn in and out of the holes until each hole has been used. Weave across, up, and down. If the yarn length gets short, just tie another piece to it.
3. When you are finished, knot the yarn through a hole and cut off any extra.

Finishing Touches

To make a more realistic-looking dreamcatcher, punch three holes on the outside of the rim. Invite each child to tie a length of yarn to each hole. Help her lay a feather along each yarn length; then wrap it with tape to secure. Sweet dreams!

Weaving

"Webby" Good!

Even the youngest artists can weave these adorable webs!

Materials:
- class supply of 7" black paper plates
- lengths of yarn
- masking tape

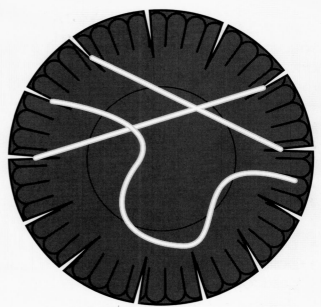

Setup:
1. Snip slits at equal intervals around the rim of each plate.
2. Arrange the materials for easy student access.

Process:

Have each child follow these steps to use the weaving process:
1. Slip one end of a length of yarn into a slit. Tape it to the back of the plate.
2. Weave the yarn by pulling it tautly across the plate and securing it in a slit on the other side. Pull the yarn across the back of the plate and up through a different slit.
3. Continue weaving the web in this manner until the yarn has nearly run out. Then pull the yarn through one last slit and tape it to the back of the plate.

Finishing Touches

Want to make these webs a bit more creepy-crawly? Consider providing each child with a plastic spider ring. Just before she finishes her weaving, have her slip the spider ring onto the yarn. Then help her complete the project by taping the yarn as described above. "Spider-ific!"

Wrapping

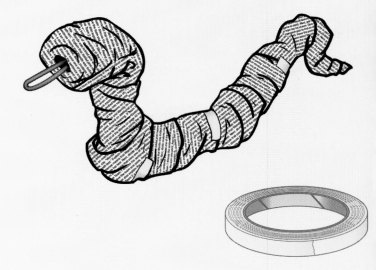

Snakes Alive!

Your youngsters will eagerly await the chance to take these slithery creations home!

Materials:
- class supply of straightened wire coat hangers
- newspapers
- masking tape
- bowls of liquid starch
- paint
- paintbrushes
- craft foam scraps
- glue

Setup:

1. Bend each coat hanger to resemble a snake as shown.
2. Arrange the newspapers, masking tape, and bowls of liquid starch for easy student access.

Process:

Have each child follow these steps to use the wrapping process:

1. Think about what kind of snake you'd like to make.
2. Wrap newspaper around your wire and secure it with tape.
3. Tear newspaper strips.
4. Dip a newspaper strip in liquid starch; then wrap it around your snake. Smooth the edges.
5. Continue wrapping the snake in this manner until you like the way it looks.
6. Set your snake aside to dry for two to three days.
7. Paint your snake. Use cool colors and add fun designs if you like.
8. Finish your snake by gluing on craft foam eyes and a tongue.

Finishing Touches

Why not turn your classroom into a herpetarium (reptile house) for a few days? Simply invite students to display their snakelike creations on long tables covered with brown or green paper and crumpled paper rocks to represent a natural habitat. "Sssuper"!

Wrapping

Wrap and Roll

These easy yet festive decorations are perfect any time of the year!

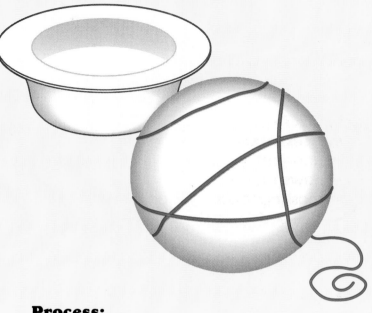

Materials:
- class supply of polystyrene foam shapes
- bowls of water-thinned glue
- lengths of colorful yarn
- glitter

Setup:
Arrange the materials for easy student access.

Process:
Have each child follow these steps to use the wrapping process:

1. Dip a length of yarn into the glue.
2. Wrap the yarn around your foam shape.
3. Repeat Steps 1 and 2 until you like the way your shape looks.
4. Sprinkle your shape with glitter.
5. Set your shape aside to dry overnight.

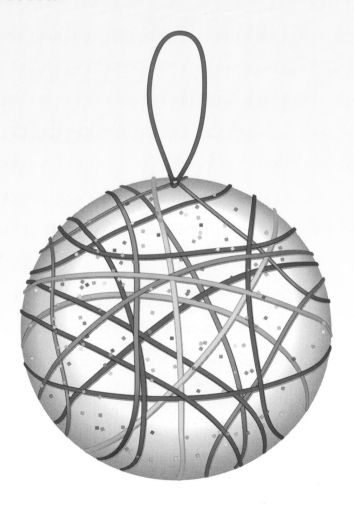

Finishing Touches

If desired, add a yarn hanger to each child's wrapped shape. Double-knot a loop in a length of yarn. Push a straight pin through the knot and into the shape. Use a dab of craft glue to secure the pin in place. Trim the leftover ends of the yarn length and hang the wrapped decoration where it can be admired by all. How pretty!

Wrapping

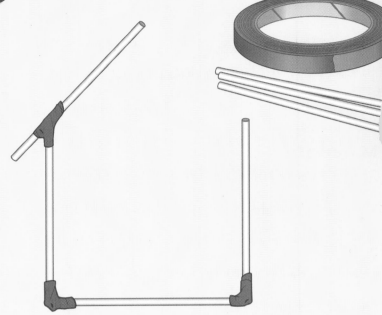

Partner Art

Find a pal and get ready to wrap a friendly sculpture or two!

Materials:
- drinking straws
- coffee stirrers
- colored masking tape

Setup:

Arrange the materials for easy student access.

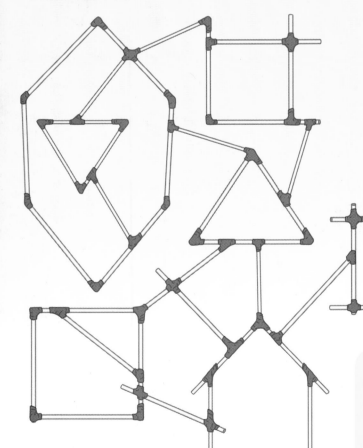

Process:

Have each pair follow these steps to use the wrapping process:

1. Decide together what you want to make.
2. Choose straws, coffee stirrers, or both to form a shape.
3. While your partner holds the straws or stirrers in place, wrap a joint of the shape with tape to secure it.
4. Taking turns holding and wrapping, repeat Step 3 until you both like the way the shape looks.

Finishing Touches

This wrapping process lends itself to a class project like no other! Invite each pair to connect its finished shape to another with more straws, stirrers, and tape. Then invite that group to connect its shape to another in the same fashion. Continue in this manner until all the shapes are incorporated. Now you have an abstract sculpture that makes a fantastic display of artistic teamwork. It's a wrap!